Original title:
Tying the World Together

Copyright © 2025 Creative Arts Management OÜ
All rights reserved.

Author: Samuel Kensington
ISBN HARDBACK: 978-1-80586-170-6
ISBN PAPERBACK: 978-1-80586-642-8

The String that Links Us

In a world of knots and bows,
We dance like socks that never know.
A thread that binds with silly flair,
Holding hands in the cosmic air.

Juggling life like wobbly clowns,
Dropping dreams and silly frowns.
Silly strings from toe to chin,
Laughter ties us thick and thin.

Giggling ribbon, tugging tight,
Knots of joy in day and night.
We skip through life, oh what a sight,
Woven close with pure delight.

So let's embrace the tangled fun,
A patchwork quilt for everyone.
Together we twirl, a goofy spree,
Stitching memories, you and me.

The Unseen Network

Look around, you might not see,
Signals bouncing like a spree.
Invisible threads pull us near,
Tickling toes, bring a cheer.

A ping here, a buzz there,
Messages floating through the air.
Sneaky squirrels, whispering trees,
Sharing secrets with the bees.

In this dance of pixel play,
Life's a game we laugh at each day.
Like a cat that chases its tail,
We're all linked in this funny trail.

So raise a toast, lift your mug,
To the network giving us a hug.
Together we prank and tease,
Boundless fun with greatest ease.

Echoes and Threads

Voices bounce like rubber balls,
Echoing through these funny halls.
Every laugh, a wave, a cheer,
We branch out, connecting here.

Threads of chatter, bright and swift,
We share our joys, that's the gift.
From silly jokes to stories grand,
Creating bonds that make us stand.

Be it a hiccup or a sneeze,
Every quirk becomes a tease.
We catch each giggle, toss it high,
Laughter soars, like birds in sky.

So grab a friend, give a shout,
In this web, there's no doubt.
Together we jive with style and grace,
Each echo a smile in this wild space.

Together We Rise

In a circus of chaos and cheer,
We juggle life from far and near.
Like mismatched shoes on the line,
With every step, we intertwine.

A dance unfolds, a cheerful scene,
Where rubber chickens feel so keen.
Hopscotch paths and silly slides,
Our joy a link that never hides.

From dizzy spins to gentle sighs,
We float like kites in bright blue skies.
Chasing rainbows, silly ties,
In this game, the fun never dies.

So throw confetti, share a grin,
In this wacky world, we all win.
Hand in hand, let's take a ride,
With laughter flowing, side by side.

The United Tapestry

In a world of fabric, we stitch and weave,
With silly threads that make us believe.
Laughter unravels, colors collide,
Creating a quilt where oddities bide.

A patchwork of quirks, so odd yet so bright,
Where socks find their partners, a peculiar sight.
Dancing with buttons, and zippers that sing,
A tapestry woven from each little thing.

Each thread tells a story, a humorous twist,
Of cats in top hats and things that don't exist.
So let's sew together with friendship's embrace,
And cover the world in this wacky space.

Though seams may unravel and fray at the ends,
We'll patch them with giggles, and call them our friends.
In this jumbled creation, our joy will be quenched,
For the crazier it gets, the more we'll be drenched.

Branches of the Global Tree

Up in the treetops, where monkeys play tricks,
Global branches sway, like a bag full of picks.
Each leaf is a story, each twig has a friend,
Swinging together, the fun has no end.

Squirrels sharing acorns, they barter and laugh,
While the wise old owl acts as the bar's staff.
Chattering birds, a symphonic delight,
In this tree of connection, all things feel right.

The roots are a party, a dance in the dirt,
Where worms do the twist, and the bugs wear their shirts.
All under the sun, the tree dances free,
A comical life in this global spree.

In this canopy world, we all intertwine,
From branches to blossoms, we merrily shine.
We'll giggle and swing, with arms open wide,
As we sway in the breeze, with nature as guide.

Resonance of Connection

Where laughter echoes from mountain to sea,
We pluck at the strings of camaraderie.
The drummer's a cat with a tambourine tail,
Playing a tune about friendship's detail.

Each note brings a chuckle, each chord is a smile,
As giggles bounce back like sound waves in style.
From city to country, the melodies flow,
Creating a symphony, don't steal the show!

The trumpets are toasters, the flutes are old spoons,
As we dance in our kitchens beneath moony balloons.
With each quirky rhythm, we all play our part,
Resonating together, a cheerful heart.

So grab a weird instrument; join in the fun,
Let's serenade life 'til the day is all done.
With chords of connection, our spirits will rise,
In this orchestra of laughter, a grand surprise.

Knotted Dreams

In the land of lost socks, where dreams tend to play,
Knots of our thoughts get tangled each day.
With rubber bands laughing and strings flying high,
We weave our ambitions beneath a wild sky.

Creativity bubbles like soda on ice,
With hiccups of humor, the sweetest of spice.
A yarn ball of wishes, an intricate mess,
Wrapped in a riddle, we giggle no less.

Unraveling dreams, a delightful big task,
As we tumble through twists, with questions to ask.
In knots of our making, we find our own way,
With smiles as our compass, come what may.

So throw on your laughter, and tie it in tight,
Let dreams lead you forward, from morning 'til night.
Each knot tells a tale, with a wink and a grin,
As we dance through the chaos, let the fun begin!

The Tapestry of Belonging

In a café, a cat sips tea,
Two birds gossip, oh so free.
The dog in a hat tells a joke,
While the goldfish laughs in a cloak.

Knitting yarn with odd designs,
A goat dives into old pines.
Socks are lost and doughnuts roll,
At this party, we're all whole.

Squirrels throw acorns like confetti,
A raccoon sings, oh so petty.
Chaos in a choreographed dance,
Who knew that beans could prance?

Weaving threads of purple and green,
This quirky crew is quite the scene.
Connected by laughs and by spills,
Creating joy is our best thrill.

One World, Many Stories

A penguin winks at a giraffe,
The elephant sneezes, what a laugh!
Stars gather round for a good tale,
As a mouse hitches a ride on a whale.

Cacti wear hats in the sun,
A snail races, thinking it's fun.
The moon cracks jokes with the sun,
While jellybeans bounce, oh what a run!

In this land where all tales mix,
Laughter shimmers like silly tricks.
Every laugh a thread, every grin,
Let's spin our fables from within.

So gather 'round, the stories flow,
From the tiniest seed to the tallest crow.
In this quirky, wondrous sphere,
Join the laughter; let's persevere.

The Echoing Ties

A frog hops in rhythm with a mouse,
Whispers travel from house to house.
A worm gets tangled in some light,
As owls gather for a night-time fright.

Laughter echoes from tree to tree,
While ants play tag with great glee.
The sound of joy is quite a tune,
Serenading the bright full moon.

In this chorus, all join in,
From the tiniest ant to the big bear's grin.
Each note ties a story to the next,
Creating a world that's quite perplexed.

When drums roll, and the goats all cheer,
Frogs croak loudly, no need to fear.
Together we laugh, together we sing,
In this echo, joy is the thing.

Unity in the Symphony

A crab plays games with a troupe of mice,
They dance together, oh so nice.
A pig on a flute lets out a song,
While the fox hums along, never wrong.

The drums of the earth beat a funny tune,
Raccoons gather 'neath the silver moon.
Marshmallow clouds drift on by,
As parakeets swoop through the sky.

Every creature with dreams to share,
Join in a zany, lively affair.
With spoon-birds stirring pots of stew,
And laughter echoing bright and true.

Together we weave a joyful sound,
In this grand symphony, love is found.
The world twirls round, a playful dance,
In our melody, let's take a chance.

The Strength of Unity

In a world where socks go missing,
One shoe can start a dance,
Countries unite, it's quite dismissing,
To let chance lead the chance.

A cat wears a hat, how absurd,
As we all join this parade,
Laughter echoes, voices stirred,
Unity is our grand charade.

With a wink and a silly grin,
We gather, strange as it sounds,
A silly dance beneath the skin,
Together, see how joy resounds!

So grab a friend, don't be late,
Join in this whimsical spree,
For unity's a curious fate,
Where all can dance—just wait and see!

The Pulse of a Global Heart

In a place where mischief thrives,
Heartbeats sync like a drum,
While penguins in tuxedos jive,
We're all here, so let's succumb.

A chicken crossed the world today,
To find its feathered mate,
With each thud and laughter sway,
Global heart, you can't be late!

Bananas wearing party hats,
Join this crazy carnival,
With every giggle, world unites,
In this pulse, we feel it all!

Let's juggle dreams and cheers so bright,
In our silly, brave embrace,
A pulse that dances, pure delight,
Connects us all in shared space!

A Circle of Hands

Round and round we hold it tight,
A circle spun from giggles raw,
With wiggly fingers, what a sight,
From Bangkok to Saint-Paul's draw.

A llama jumps, it's quite the jest,
As hands join hands and twirl about,
We're unified, but jesting best,
As laughter drowns out every doubt.

While juggling fruit and joy, oh dear,
A twist of fate can tickle, too,
With silly songs and bouts of cheer,
A circle's magic starts anew.

So pass the joy, this circus blend,
Gesture wide, let laughter soar,
In this circle, we transcend,
Hand in hand, forevermore!

Weaving Light Across the Globe

With threads of joy and silly glee,
We weave a quilt of dreams so bright,
No needle pricks, just jubilee,
As laughter lights up every night.

From North to South, our laughter sails,
Like jellybeans on a sunny spree,
In silly costumes and fairy tales,
We craft a world where all can be!

A juggling act—a twisty thread,
Balloon animals float on air,
Through knots of fun, no tears are shed,
Together we craft a vibrant flair.

Let colors dance and mingle bright,
As we all join the tapestry,
Weaving happiness by sheer delight,
In this fabric, we all agree!

The Cord of Compassion

In a world that spins like a dizzy cat,
Everyone's looking for a friendly chat.
With compassion wrapped in a silly bow,
We laugh at the troubles that come and go.

A hug is like duct tape, holding us tight,
Mending our hearts, making wrong things right.
With a wink and a grin, we lift heavy loads,
Creating a bond that lightens our roads.

So share a cookie, or just a kind word,
Laughter flies high like a colorful bird.
For every excuse to giggle and cheer,
Builds bridges that shine when the skies aren't clear.

When life gives you lemons, squeeze on a friend,
Together we'll blend and our laughter won't end.
In this crazy circus, we sip on good cheer,
Creating connections where joy is sincere.

One Breath, Many Voices

A chorus of giggles fills the bright sky,
From whispers and secrets that float up high.
Each laugh is a note in our symphony sweet,
We dance on the breeze with our silly little feet.

Like balloons in a parade, we color the gray,
Every smile a banner that's here to stay.
With voices united, we sing out our cheer,
Creating a ruckus that everyone hears.

In this playful carnival where joy has begun,
Each chatter and chortle is all kinds of fun.
The world sings along, in a merry ballet,
With every connection, we brighten the day.

So raise up your cup, let's toast our delight,
In this whimsical choir that echoes the night.
With laughter as glue, we'll stick together,
Through ups and downs, like light as a feather.

Shared Horizons

On the edge of a cliff where the sun likes to play,
We gather our dreams and dance the day away.
Each sunset a brushstroke, painted with care,
In hues of our stories that float in the air.

With binoculars peering at our neighbor's quirks,
We laugh at the foibles and all the hard works.
In the blend of our lives, we're a mix and a match,
Creating a landscape that none can dispatch.

When clouds gather round and the sky turns to grey,
We tickle each other to keep worries at bay.
With a smirk and a wink, we stand side by side,
As friends in this journey, like a joyous ride.

So raise a straw hat as we bask in the glow,
To horizons we share, where fun lives and grows.
In this vibrant bazaar, we'll paint with a dream,
Where giggles are currency and laughter's the theme.

Entwined Destinies

In a tapestry woven from threads of delight,
We dance through the fabric, our futures in sight.
With each silly mishap, we coil and we twirl,
Creating a story that's bright as a pearl.

Like gum on the sidewalk, we stick through it all,
Through stumbles and tumbles, we answer the call.
In the circus of life where we juggle and play,
Our destinies sparkle in a comical way.

With mismatched socks and a grin that won't fade,
We spin through adventures, each moment well-played.
In this playful mosaic, we paint with a thrill,
Holding hands with our dreams, we wander at will.

So let's raise a toast to the paths that entwine,
In laughter and friendship, so warm and divine.
With chuckles as anchors, we sail ever free,
Building bonds that are silly, but endlessly glee.

Knots of Kinship

In my backyard, a dog chased a cat,
While a squirrel laughed, wearing a hat.
Grandma's yarn tangled in a bush,
Even the goldfish gave a little push.

Cards formed castles, wildly they fell,
Tea cups danced, oh, what a swell!
A cousin's joke turned the room red,
As laughter spun like a thread.

Every phone call is a wacky affair,
With Aunt Sue's gossip and Uncle's despair.
Mismatched socks, the fashion today,
Bringing us close in a quirky way.

Together we'll spin, with stories to tell,
In knots of kinship, all is well!

Weaving a Global Tapestry

A panda in pajamas sips on green tea,
While a toucan sings, looking snazzy.
From Australia to Peru, from sea to land,
We share our snacks, isn't that grand?

A dance-off breaks out near the Eiffel,
With tourists joining in, it's quite a trial!
Global flavors on a pizza pie,
With pineapple topping, oh me, oh my!

A selfie with llamas, how very chic,
With funny faces and laughter unique.
From different corners, we pile on quick,
Spinning our tales, it does the trick.

In this vibrant weave, we find our place,
Lively and loud, with cheer on our face!

Bridges of Understanding

Two goats on a bridge look quite at ease,
One's chewing straw, the other's a tease.
They argue about which side is best,
Creating a bridge from their funny quest.

Pigs in the air, flying high on a whim,
While the chickens plot, their future looks grim.
They collaborate on a grand escape,
In a world made of laughter, we're all shaped.

With mismatched shoes, we hop to the beat,
Creating a rhythm that's hard to compete.
In this bumpy ride, we share a smile,
Bridges are built, but just with style!

So let's bridge the gap with silly delight,
As we waddle along, everything feels right!

Interlaced Souls

Two squirrels chitchat in my old oak tree,
Swap war stories about who stole their pea.
A bird interrupts, with a song to share,
While ants march in, totally unaware.

A mix-up in the kitchen, flour in the air,
Mom's trying to bake, but it's everywhere!
The dog steals a biscuit, makes a grand dash,
Yet here we all smile, in a comical clash.

Sock puppet championships, who will compete?
With mismatched footwear, what a funny feat!
Together we frolic, no worries to keep,
In this joyful mess, our hearts take a leap.

With knotted connections, our laughter takes flight,
In the game of life, we shine oh-so-bright!

Converging Currents

In a café where the barista sings,
Coffee swirls do crazy things.
Lattes dance, a foamy cheer,
Milk and sugar waltz near here.

The croissant giggles, butter flies,
Donuts wink with sugary eyes.
Sips of chatter, giggles bright,
In this blend, all feels just right.

Around the table, friends unite,
Sharing tales, what a delight!
Jokes like sparks, they whizz and zoom,
Creating joy, heroes in the room.

Laughter spills like endless streams,
In this chaos, brewing dreams.
With every sip, a new idea,
In this mix, there's love and cheer!

Tying Threads of Kindness

In a fabric shop, colors clash,
Sewing skills? Oh, look at that flash!
Needles dance, the bobbins spin,
   Creating smiles from within.

A quilt of giggles, stitched so tight,
With patches of joy, a lively sight.
Sewing circles, worlds collide,
   Friendship woven, side by side.

Patterns twist in vibrant hues,
Sharing fabric, sharing blues.
Laughter echoes with every thread,
   In this tapestry, happiness spread.

At the end, a blanket bold,
Each stitched laugh, a story told.
Warmed by kindness, draped in light,
With every thread, our hearts ignited!

The Web of Life

Spiders knitting in the trees,
Waving to the bumblebees.
In the garden, a funny sight,
Webs of giggles, pure delight.

Flies buzzing on a silver string,
Chasing laughs, oh what a fling!
Ladybugs join the happy dance,
In this web, they take a chance.

Wiggly worms and ants parade,
Making tunnels, plans well laid.
Every creature, big and small,
In this web, together we all.

In the dawn, the dew drops gleam,
As the world wakes, it feels like a dream.
With every thread, a tale anew,
In this web, there's room for you!

A Harmonious Spectrum

Colors clash in a painter's spree,
Splashes of laughter, wild and free.
Rainbows tremble with a giggle,
As artists play and doodles wiggle.

Bright yellow sings with cheerful cheer,
While blue makes waves, oh dear, oh dear!
Crimson leaps with fiery flair,
They swirl and dance without a care.

Palette mixes, spills in love,
Like a chorus from above.
Each hue brings a brand new tune,
Creating smiles from sun to moon.

In this riot, colors arise,
Crafting visions that mesmerize.
Under this spectrum, hearts convene,
In this fun, we craft the scene!

Love in Every Stitch

In every stitch, there's a tale,
Of socks that dance, and ties that sail.
A button lost, a thread in a knot,
Each quirky fix, a giggle forgot.

While sewing patches on my jeans,
I found a cat, or so it seems.
With every tug and every whine,
My fabric turns to a circus line.

A hat that slips, a scarf that flops,
When crafting joy, the laughter hops.
Sewing friends, a playful crew,
Each crazy quilt, a laugh anew.

So grab your bobbins, don't delay,
Let's sew our jokes with thread today!
For every stitch, a silly cheer,
In fabric joy, we hold so dear.

Patches of Togetherness

I found a patch, quite round and bright,
It danced along in sheer delight.
A circle here, a square up high,
Each piece joins in with a sly goodbye.

With mismatched colors, we all collide,
As laughter blooms, we take a ride.
A patchwork quilt, it's quite the sight,
A blend of chaos, pure delight!

A pocket sewn with secret thread,
Holds all the laughter in our heads.
Together stitched, we won't unbind,
In every laugh, new hugs we find.

So grab your fabric, come join the spree,
Creating laughter, just you and me!
In every patch, a story's spun,
Together in jest, our hearts are one.

The Knot of Understanding

Behold the knot, a twist so grand,
It ties together every hand.
With double loops and a silly slip,
It keeps us close, a friendship trip.

A sailor's knot, or maybe two,
It holds our tales, and even stew.
When things get tangled, and we can't see,
We laugh it off, you and me.

So when you're stuck, just give a tug,
The laughter flows like a warm, soft hug.
We'll knot our troubles, and braid some fun,
In this crazy life, we'll always run.

With every twist, there's a joke or two,
In every loop, I cherish you.
The knots we share will never fray,
In this crazy dance, let's sway away!

The Knots of Humanity

We twist and turn, a dance so grand,
In life's wild party, hand in hand.
With shoes untied and laughter loud,
We trip together, a joyful crowd.

From every corner, quirks emerge,
While we all stumble, we still converge.
A tangled mess, but all in fun,
Knots of humor, we're never done.

In mismatched socks and silly hats,
We're just a bunch of playful rats.
In crowded rooms, we weave our tales,
And ride the waves like iron sails.

So let's embrace this knotty scheme,
With every giggle, we live the dream.
The chaos binds us, ties anew,
With laughter bright, our hearts break through.

Binding the Distant Stars

A cat's meow in the midst of night,
As we reel in stars with all our might.
They shine so far, yet feel so near,
With each silly face, we draw them here.

Galaxies dance while we juggle dreams,
In cosmic chaos, nothing's as it seems.
We'll wrap the moon with rainbow string,
And make it spin while we all sing.

Our friendship stretches, like comets blaze,
Through tangled laughter, we weave our ways.
With every chuckle, a star is born,
In this great universe, we're never torn.

So let's collide in a swirling spree,
As jokes and giggles set us free.
With every bond, a new light flows,
Together we shine, as everyone knows.

The Weave of Time

Tick-tock goes the clock, don't fall asleep,
As we stitch seconds, a pile we keep.
In threads of laughter, we craft our fate,
With every snicker, we celebrate.

We gather memories, a silky swatch,
With colors bright that never botch.
The fabric of life, with seams so tight,
In every hug, we spark delight.

A tapestry rich, a quilt of cheer,
We knot our stories, year by year.
With silly puns and funny rhymes,
We dance through the weave of endless times.

So grab a needle, come join the fun,
In the stitch of life, we've just begun.
With every thread, a bond we find,
A masterpiece of the joyful kind.

A Heartbeat Shared

Bouncing hearts in a quirky beat,
We share our laughs, a rhythmic cheat.
With every giggle, our pulses race,
In this wild dance, we find our place.

From goofy games to silly faces,
In this mad world, everyone embraces.
We skip through puddles, we leap with glee,
Synchronizing joy, just you and me.

With beat-box rhythms and playful twirls,
Our laughter spins and endlessly swirls.
In this heartbeat shared, we find the glow,
A comedy act in the life's grand show.

So join the fun, don't hold it back,
With laughter's spark, we'll never lack.
Together we dance, a lively fare,
In the heartbeat shared, we truly care.

The Network of Existence

In a town where squirrels dance,
And pigeons hold a meeting stance,
Cats wear hats and shout with glee,
While dogs discuss philosophy.

The mayor is a rabbit bold,
With tales of adventures untold,
They share a drink of acorn tea,
In this network, wild and free.

Neighbors hug, though trees stand tall,
Raccoons sneak snacks, they love to brawl,
Life spins like a carnival ride,
With laughter echoing far and wide.

So gather 'round, both young and old,
In this odd place where fun unfolds,
It's a web of joys, quirky and strange,
Where friendships bloom, and lives exchange.

An Embrace Across Cultures

A taco sings with curry flair,
While sushi winks with spicy air,
Gelato joins the conga line,
As pizza twirls with a glass of wine.

Fried rice chats with a baguette,
Each flavor's waltz, a lively duet,
They scoff at borders, laugh at rules,
In their embrace, there are no fools.

From tacos to dolmas, all unite,
Through savory dreams that dance at night,
They share laughter in a pot so wide,
With ingredients melding inside each stride.

So swirl around the globe with glee,
Find humor in each recipe,
For together, they craft a feast,
A world of joy, to say the least.

Knitted Together

A scarf for the cat, and gloves for the dog,
With yarn that flew like a friendly fog,
Each stitch a laugh, every twist a cheer,
As needles tap dance—what a sight here!

Old Grandmother's chair creaks in delight,
While turtles model sweaters, oh what a sight!
They strut on the runway, so proud and spry,
Even the fish wave as they swim by.

A patchwork quilt of colors bright,
Wraps up the moon, hugs the night,
Each thread a story, laughter's embrace,
In this crafted world, there's always space.

So grab your yarn, and join the fun,
In this warm web, we all have won,
With knitted smiles that never fray,
Together we bloom, day by day.

The Unseen Thread

A spider spins with a goofy grin,
As ants march with their tiny kin,
They weave a path up to the moon,
Singing their oddball, merry tune.

A rainbow pops, like a jack-in-the-box,
While clouds put on their silly frocks,
Each color giggles, bright and bold,
In this web of wonder, life untold.

From starry nights to the sunlit dawn,
They thread their tales, interwoven, drawn,
With laughter threading through the air,
Binding all, we dance without a care.

So join the dance, don't be late,
In this thread of smiles, let's celebrate,
For though unseen, it is truly there,
In this jolly strand we all can share.

Embracing the Web of Life

In a web of shoelaces, we dance and trip,
Knotted friendships from our crazy trip.
A cat that meows loud while we try to sing,
Makes squirrels laugh as they hear us swing.

Our emails fly like paper planes,
Texting puns about our daily pains.
We juggle our dreams like fruit in a bowl,
With laughter and joy, we share a whole role.

The sun's shining bright, but the rain gives a wink,
We paint our troubles with colors that blink.
Life's a circus, with monkeys in hats,
Swinging from chaos, laughing with chitchats.

Connecting our quirks like mismatched socks,
Even the clock seems to dance 'round the blocks.
So here's to the chaos, let's raise a toast,
To the tangled web life's given us most!

The Common Thread

Two left feet in a dance class unite,
While someone's lost their pants full of fright.
Threading through moments, we stitch and we laugh,
With jokes like our grandma's fine knitted scarf.

We trade friendly jabs from across the room,
Like socks that get lost in the laundry's dark gloom.
A cat on a keyboard, oh what a sight,
Typing new words as it dances in flight.

Fast food and lattes, we meet to unwind,
Sharing odd stories of friends left behind.
We're a patchwork quilt, in strange colors sewn,
Making memories from moments unknown.

So let's poke the bear and tickle some toes,
In this quilt of life, anything goes!
Come join the chaos, with laughter we thread,
In the fabric of friendship, we joyfully spread.

Echoes of Togetherness

Once a tweet from a bird made life feel right,
As echoes of laughter danced into the night.
We juggle our thoughts like water balloons,
And burst into giggles, beneath silly moons.

The coffee shop's buzzing with dreams on a roll,
As we toast to mishaps that fill up our bowl.
A parade of ducks in a single line strut,
We trip over giggles, then end in a rut.

As echoes bounce back, let's dance to the drum,
With spoons in our pockets, and patience feels numb.
We photobomb moments with laughter and cheer,
As a cat takes the stage and steals our next beer.

Join in the chorus, let's belt out a song,
With harmonies crazy, fumbling along.
In the echoes of joy, we find our sweet place,
In the laughter of life, there's room for all grace.

Hand in Hand Across the Globe

With mismatched gloves, we wander the scene,
Two clumsy penguins, a sight quite serene.
Hand in hand, we juggle the joys that we find,
Like lost socks on a quest, forever entwined.

We sip from coconuts under a bright sun,
While someone tells jokes, oh, aren't we just fun?
Tacos and laughter, a salsa delight,
Flipping our woes in this playful flight.

Through mud on our shoes, we slog and we dance,
Making each trip feel like a romping romance.
Hand in hand, we summit the peaks of the day,
With smiles and giggles, come what may.

So grab a balloon and let's float through the skies,
With each twist and turn, we see the sun rise.
Together we wander, share odd bits of fate,
In this globetrotting adventure, laughter won't wait!

Connections in the Cosmos

In a world of mismatched socks,
We find our friends, they're just like rocks.
Planetary giggles in the air,
Aliens wondering, 'Is anyone there?'

With spaghetti strings and random marks,
Drawing lines to all the snarky sharks.
Health nuts bouncing like silly bunnies,
Flipping pancakes, making fun of honeys!

Through the bubbles of our shared delight,
We craft connections that feel just right.
Dancing like lobsters on the moon,
Bringing laughter, a hilarious tune!

So let's hold hands with our cosmic pals,
Dressed as chickens, and joyful gals.
In this quirky party of fabulous flair,
We're all just threads, floating in the air!

Woven Whispers

Whispers weave like a game of tag,
In a sea of laughter, we all brag.
Sticky notes flutter, like leaves in a breeze,
Painting our chatter with giggles and tease.

A cat in a hat joins us for tea,
Throwing confetti, 'Oh, look at me!'
Juggling oranges while riding a bike,
Watch out for custard, it's not what you like!

Through crazy antics and silly rhymes,
We connect like clockwork, through strange times.
A crossword puzzle without a clue,
Finding odd answers, just me and you.

So tie your shoelaces, don't trip on a joke,
Let's leap together, like a frog in a yoke.
With every giraffe that dances with flair,
We're all neighbors, in this odd, funny square!

The Language of Kinship

In a world of giggles and pancake battles,
We speak in giggles, not in rattles.
A wink to the left, a nod to the right,
Synchronized dances that last through the night.

Each barbecue joke is a thread in our quilt,
With sauce-covered hugs that make laughter spill.
Puns fly around like balloons in the sky,
When the dog joins in, we can't help but cry!

We trade all our secrets like jellybeans,
Laughing as we can, behind the scenes.
Timid turtles even break out with glee,
In this crazy circus of you and me.

The language we share is quirky and fun,
With pratfalls and mischief, we all come undone.
So grab a megaphone, shout it out loud,
In this wild kinship, we're all so proud!

Knots of Empathy

Tangled in laughter, like shoes in a knot,
We notice the silly, forget what we've sought.
Worried about dinner? Let's start a food fight!
Making merry messes under the moonlight.

With yarn that's unraveled across the whole floor,
We connect while we giggle, running out the door.
High-fives and weird faces that lighten the load,
Like bubbles in lemonade, we're ready to explode!

Each fidgety squawk of a bird on a wire,
Brings stories that soar, and never expire.
Stitching our joys with zany delight,
Knots of empathy that twirl through the night.

So grab a balloon, and float high above,
With friendships that shine, like the stars we love.
In this amusing tapestry we share and create,
We're bound by our laughter, it's never too late!

A Network of Light

In a land where bulbs flicker and glow,
Socks and lights dance in a silly show.
The toaster's in chat with the old TV,
Making breakfast while streaming a spree.

A fridge and a blender engage in a jest,
Competing on who makes the best breakfast.
Cups spill the gossip, plates join the fun,
Connecting our laughter when the day's begun.

The clock watches closely, ticks filled with glee,
Reminding the kettle, 'Don't spill on me!'
While the broom sweeps in, spinning a tale,
Of how the mighty dust bunny set sail.

So here's to the gadgets, in mischief they dive,
In this bright network, we all feel alive!
Each blink and each beep, a quirky delight,
Uniting us all, in a dance of pure light.

Threads of Hope

In a world where spaghetti tangles anew,
Forks tell tales, and spoons join too.
A cat in a hat claims the thread as its own,
While laughter unravels from each tasty scone.

Knitting our joy, those old yarns collide,
With socks that mismatch, but still wear with pride.
A quilt with patches that wiggle and sway,
Stitched with the laughter of yesterday.

Buttons have secrets, they giggle and cheer,
As zippers and laces all share a beer.
They toast to the moments, both wild and sweet,
In this patchwork of smiles, we find our beat.

So dance with the threads that connect us today,
With stitches of joy guiding our way.
Together we weave in this whimsical dance,
Creating connections that leave nothing to chance.

Stitching Our Stories

In a realm where tales are stitched with delight,
A fabric of friendship shines ever so bright.
The buttons all chatter, exchanging a wink,
While the scissors join in, ready to think.

Every patch is a memory, each fabric a song,
Stitched side by side, we have all belonged.
A needle pokes fun, with a pointy jest,
Sewing up moments where laughter's the guest.

Threads of our journeys, tangled and wild,
In this funny quilt, we're all like a child.
With stories that twist and turn like a yarn,
We stitch all our dreams under the stars.

So gather your pieces and let's all unite,
In this comical fabric woven so tight.
Together we'll laugh, as we sway to a tune,
Stitching our stories beneath the bright moon.

Connected Through the Seasons

When autumn leaves dance in a swirling laugh,
Pumpkins join forces, sharing their craft.
The winter snowmen gather in cheer,
With carrots and hats, they spread winter's magic here.

Spring brings the blooms, with a chittering sound,
Bunnies and birds all gather around.
They hop and they chirp, sharing the news,
Of flowers and sunshine, joys they can't lose.

Summer arrives with a splash in the pool,
Where beach balls and floaties make every rule.
Grilling and chilling, it's a party galore,
With friends from each season bursting through the door.

Thus cycles our friendship, through weather and fun,
Connected like sunshine, moon, and the sun.
In every season, in laughter we play,
Each moment together, brightening the day.

Threads of Unity

In a cafe, two spoons collide,
Coffee splashes, oh what a ride!
Laughter echoes, a united cheer,
Sticky notes dance, as friends draw near.

A cat on a leash, chasing a mouse,
While neighbors argue, what's wrong with the house?
A tumble of giggles, all tangled in fun,
In this crazy world, we're all just one.

Socks mismatched in a drawer so deep,
Together we laugh, together we leap.
With every blunder, every silly mistake,
We know side by side, there's always a break.

So let's grab our snacks, make a giant mess,
Unravel the tension, forget all the stress.
Hearts and giggles, a melody sweet,
In quirky adventures, we find our heartbeat.

The Fabric of Connection

Quilts of stories, sewn with delight,
Each patch a memory, colorful and bright.
Grandma's old fabric, a tale we unfold,
Stitched with laughter, like treasures of gold.

Buttons and zippers all go for a trip,
The pockets are laughing, oh what a blip!
Threads of old jokes, every fiber a giggle,
In this fabric of life, we swish and we wiggle.

Mix up the patterns, let chaos reign,
A dance of connections, we cannot contain.
From silly mishaps, to bundled delight,
Together we'll shine, like stars in the night.

So gather your stitches, your yarns, and your jokes,
In this tapestry woven, let's laugh till we choke.
With every twirl, every meme that we send,
We find in this fabric, we're all just a blend.

Knotted Journeys

Maps made of spaghetti, what's that in store?
A trip of confusion, who knows what's in store?
Navigating laughs, oh where will we go?
Every turn a chuckle, in the winds that blow.

Around the corner, a sign upside-down,
Tangled in laughter as we twirl around town.
A donut-shaped planet, who knew what we'd find?
With every new knot, we expand our own mind.

Chasing our tails, we stumble and fall,
Yet every misstep, brings giggles for all.
Wrapped in the nonsense, together we scurry,
In the knot of the journey, there's no need to hurry.

So let's pack our bags, filled with crazy and cheer,
Traveling in circles, with nary a fear.
With every mishap, a new tale is spun,
In this knotted adventure, we're all having fun.

Weaving Dreams into Reality

In a loom of wishes, we pull and we tug,
Weaved with our dreams, it fits like a snug.
Snipping at worries, we chuckle and cheer,
With every new thread, our hopes reappear.

A giraffe in a hat, sewing hats on the sly,
While ducks in a row are learning to fly.
The fabric of laughter, stitched with delight,
Brings joy to our visions, oh what a sight!

Patchwork of colors, our imaginations soar,
Every zany idea opens up the door.
With yarns of madness, we twirl and we dance,
In a world full of whimsy, who wouldn't take a chance?

The more we create, the stranger it seems,
Connecting the dots in our wildest of dreams.
So let's grab those fabrics, spin tales from the thread,
In this playful adventure, let laughter be spread.

Bridges Over Distances

With rubber bands and silly strings,
We stretch our laughs, oh how it swings.
From here to there, a wobbly dance,
We send our jokes, let's take a chance.

A paper plane with messages bold,
Flies past the cat, who thinks it's gold.
We send our quirks across the way,
Just to chuckle at our play.

A yodel here, a whistle there,
Our quirky bonds float through the air.
Like spaghetti tossed on a plate,
We mix our joys, never too late.

So grab a frog, or a rubber duck,
We'll bounce around, like crazy luck.
In this vast world, we laugh and sing,
Our wild connections, a bouncy swing.

Together in the Silence

In quiet rooms, we share our snacks,
With whispers soft and silly hacks.
An echo here, a giggle there,
We burst the silence with joyful air.

A look, a nod, the chocolate's shared,
With secret smiles, nobody's scared.
In hushed tones, stories come alive,
Like squirrels planning, we connive.

A sneeze disrupts our thoughtful pause,
And laughter roars, like crowds with applause.
In silence, bonds so gently weave,
Our fun-filled moments, hard to believe.

So here we sit, with snacks galore,
In quietude, we laugh some more.
Together in the hush we find,
The funniest ties by hearts entwined.

Threads of Light

Floating bubbles in the sun,
Each one giggles, having fun.
A tangle here, a twirl there,
A ribbon of laughter fills the air.

Like glow sticks at a midnight bash,
We dance like fireflies, flash after flash.
One silly face, one happy grin,
The threads of joy wrap us in.

When shadows stretch at the end of day,
Our stories light the dark away.
Like kites in a breeze, we rise so high,
Our glow uniting, reaching the sky.

So let's glow bright, with hearts so light,
In this funny dance, we'll be alright.
With threads of giggles bright and bold,
Our laughter, a tapestry of gold.

The Circle of Life

In circles round, we spin and twirl,
Chasing our tails in a silly whirl.
A pie-shaped laugh, a donut hug,
Together we squeeze, in this snug rug.

Like hula hoops, we sway and bend,
Our joy in motion, never to end.
A knock-knock joke, the punchline flies,
We roll in laughter, a sweet surprise.

With every loop, we share a grin,
The circle tightens, let the fun begin.
A merry-go-round of quirky tales,
In this dance of life, our love prevails.

So round and round, we laugh and play,
In this circle of joy, we'll stay.
With funny ties, we're hand in hand,
Together we make our silly stand.

Nurturing the Collective Spirit

In a park, a juggler jests,
While pigeons do their silly quests.
A dog slips, grabs a clown's big shoe,
Laughter echoes, a joyful brew.

Neighbors mix their BBQs,
With unexpected veggie stews.
A cat steals the last hot dog,
As kids chase it in a fog.

Friends play cards, chaos ensues,
Elbows bump, and laughter brews.
A wild twist, a game gone wrong,
Where everyone ends up in song.

Together, we spin this tale,
In fun and frolic, we won't fail.
For in our quirks and silly art,
We nurture joy—that's where we start.

Ties That Bind

A squirrel steals a picnic snack,
While laughter tumbles down the track.
A kite gets stuck in a tall tree,
Now it's a bird's own bungee spree!

A pair of socks, mismatched for sure,
Forms a dance with silliness pure.
As umbrellas flip in a sudden gust,
We giggle and find it's a must!

Neighbors argue who fell first,
In a hose fight, how could it burst?
Old friends compete in a pie-eating race,
With whipped cream smiles, what a face!

Though life can twist in winding ways,
These quirky scenes brighten our days.
The ties we share, no matter how strange,
Bring joy and laughs that will never change.

Interwoven Journeys

Two travelers meet on a busy street,
With mismatched shoes, it's quite the feat.
They swap tales of blunders and trysts,
As come the hiccups, adventure persists!

A dog and a cat play chess in the sun,
Their rivalry's always just for fun.
A rooster crows at an unsuspecting crew,
Jumping and squawking, they giggle anew!

With backpacks full of oddities found,
They share stories that know no bound.
A lost map leads to ice cream delights,
As silly scoops become wild flight nights.

Life's chords are strummed, each laugh a note,
In this symphony, we all gloat.
Together we roam, no plans in hand,
In the laughter of life, we take a stand.

A Mosaic of Togetherness

In a bustling café, the chatter flows,
A barista slips—oh, how it shows!
A coffee spill leads to cheers and grins,
As muffins take flight, and laughter wins.

A dance-off breaks in the grocery aisle,
Dazed shoppers join in, smiling all the while.
With carts full of snacks and silly hats,
They twirl and spin like joyful sprats.

A tangle of cats in a yarn shop spree,
Paws and threads knot in pure glee.
A treehouse fort, made for all,
Where children laugh and the grown-ups fall.

In every moment, a spark we find,
In laughter and joy, we're intertwined.
A artwork of fun on this crazy ride,
In the mosaic of life, we take pride.

Bonds Beyond Borders

A squirrel in Spain, whispers to bees,
Pigeons in Paris dance with the trees.
Llamas wear hats, leaping with glee,
While turtles in hats sip green tea.

In Hong Kong, cats throw wild parties,
While dogs in Berlin trade sweet carties.
Frogs in a band sing jazz by the bay,
And everyone laughs in their own goofy way.

Elephants juggle in circus delight,
As zebras groove under the moonlight.
Cows create memes that go viral fast,
In this world of quirks, no fun is ever last.

So grab your passport, dance with a goat,
Join in the fun, we'll all happily float.
With friends from afar, our hearts won't shiver,
We'll laugh and connect, sharing joy forever.

The Interwoven Dream

A pickle in London thinks he's a star,
While waffles in Brussels sing tunes from afar.
A cat with a sombrero, wow what a sight,
Spreading joy across every day and night.

Fish in a bowl play chess by the glass,
While snails in pajamas stroll through the grass.
Each critter's a comic, each laugh's a delight,
Connecting through humor, oh what a sight!

Parrots in places where no one can hear,
Crack jokes in the gardens that cradle good cheer.
While goats wear sunglasses, oh what a craze,
In this woven dream, we all share the rays.

So come grab a smile, let's tickle the air,
We'll dance 'round the globe without a single care.
With laughter our tether, we jump and we gleam,
In this silly adventure, we're living the dream.

Threads of Harmony

Socks in a drawer scheme a grand escape,
To build a parade in a fresh landscape.
With apples and oranges forming a band,
They sway to the rhythm of a fruit-filled land.

The ants in a line, plan a sweet parade,
While froggies in boots hop and invade.
Dancing with ducks, they twirl on the grass,
Creating a burst of fun, oh so fast!

Kangaroos jive with a flair and a hop,
Whales serenade while the seabirds bop.
In this charming mess of giggles and glee,
These are the threads that connect you and me.

So gather your pals, with a grin on display,
Let's weave our lives, come what may.
With laughter as glue and love as the thread,
We'll forge a connection that won't be misread.

Constellations of Connection

Stars in pajamas gossip at night,
While comets play catch in the soft moonlight.
A hedgehog in glasses reads jokes from a book,
While fireflies twinkle with a magical look.

Balloons hold meetings at the skies' great height,
As clouds joke around, keeping things light.
The puppies and kittens all form a club,
To share their secrets and start a hub.

Bubbles float free, making everyone laugh,
With astronauts giggling, joining the path.
And so it unfolds, this cosmic ballet,
Where joy's in the air, come what may.

So let's raise a toast, to the quirky and bright,
To friendships that soar like a kite in flight.
In this universe grand, we shine and we play,
Creating connections that brighten our day.

The Symphony of Togetherness

In a land where socks go free,
And every fridge holds a glee,
The banjos strum on muffin tops,
As giggles float like fizzy pops.

With noodles dancing, twirling high,
And donuts jumping, oh my my!
A marching band of rubber shoes,
In funny hats, they chase the blues.

A chorus made of clinking spoons,
Together sing beneath the moons,
They jiggle, waltz, and laugh with flair,
A symphony beyond compare.

So let's all bust a silly move,
In this dance of joy, we groove,
For the world is funny, bright, and bold,
In shared moments, our hearts unfold.

A Network of Hearts

A jester's hat on every head,
As laughter weaves like a warm spread,
We're knitting smiles, all in a row,
With silly games that steal the show.

A cat in a tie, what a delight,
With wiggly tails, they bring the light,
A network spun with hugs and cheer,
Where every heart is bound to steer.

With jellybeans as currency,
Trading giggles, oh can you see?
A web of fun, it stretches wide,
As friends in laughter side by side.

So join the party, grab a plate,
With cake and jokes, we celebrate,
In this network full of charm,
Together's where we raise the alarm!

Global Stitches

With patches bright, we stitch the night,
A quilt of dreams, all tucked in tight,
A penguin dances on a log,
While chickens lead the morning fog.

A rainbow's thread, it loops and twirls,
As giggles ripple, winds unfurl,
The earth's a fabric, vibrant, fun,
In every corner, threads we've spun.

The stitches! Oh, they twist and bind,
A quilt of laughter, one of a kind,
With every tug, a funny tale,
In colors bright, we set our sail.

So grab a thread, let's stitch away,
With hiccups, dances, come what may,
In laughter, love, our hearts rejoice,
A jolly quilt, let's all make noise!

Unity in Diversity

In all our quirks, we find the dance,
With pineapple hats, we take a chance,
A ball of yarn, it rolls with grace,
As we all juggle in this space.

With kooky dances from afar,
And silly jokes that raise the bar,
A melting pot of giggles bright,
Where everyone can join the light.

From every nook, we gather round,
With funny faces, joy unbound,
We flip the script, it's plain to see,
In diverse fun, we all agree.

So here's a toast to every heart,
In this wild play, we'll never part,
Together we create a scene,
In laughter's arms, life stays serene.

Paths Intertwined

In a tangle of shoes, we stumble and glide,
Each step echoes laughter, side by side.
The world spins in circles, we can't find our way,
Yet together we dance, come what may.

A cat that keeps sneezing, a dog wearing socks,
We trip over penguins, and chase silly clocks.
Our journeys converge in the strangest of styles,
With giggles and gaffes that go on for miles.

Through puddles we splash, as we flirt with our fate,
A burger in hand, we navigate late.
Around every corner, a twist or a turn,
With maps made of dreams, it's together we learn.

In this maze of mishaps, we share every fall,
With croissants and coffee and friends for them all.
So here's to the chaos, let's raise a toast loud,
With ties of hilarity, we're lost in the crowd.

A Fabric of Dreams

Stitching our thoughts with a thread made of cheer,
We mix up our patterns, no need for a seer.
Buttons and ruffles, a hat on a cat,
This cloak of confusion, oh, where are we at?

A quilt of adventures, a patchwork of fun,
We'll wear mismatched socks, united as one.
With each quirky seam, and each silly patch,
Our memories woven, no moment to scratch.

The world flits and flutters in colors so bright,
As we weave through the chaos, weaving day into night.
A spritz of confetti, a sprinkle of glee,
In this fabric of laughter, we all feel so free.

Like yarn on a spindle, we twist and we shout,
Embracing the hiccups that life's all about.
So here's to the mix-ups, the laughter and seams,
In the fabric we share, we fulfill all our dreams.

Harmony's Embrace

In a band made of blunders, we play the wrong tune,
With a kazoo and a spoon, we'll reach for the moon.
Discordant yet joyful, our rhythm's a ride,
In the symphony's chaos, we find a sweet stride.

With hiccups and chuckles, we serenade life,
Adding humor to troubles, no room for the strife.
A tap dance on tables, a flub in the song,
With laughter the glue that helps us get along.

The colors collide in a dance that's absurd,
As we spin through each mishap, we'll sing every word.
A chant of the silly, the wild and the whacky,
In harmony's embrace, we get a bit tacky.

So let's twirl through this world, with a wink and a grin,
In every odd note, let the fun now begin.
For in the sweet discord, there's magic to find,
In the laughter we share, our hearts are entwined.

Global Heartstrings

From the corners of the globe, we pull at our ties,
With kite strings of jokes that float up to the skies.
A tug here, a giggle, and suddenly swoosh,
We're flying together, in one single whoosh.

With balloons and parades, a carnival flair,
We juggle our woes in the midair, beware!
The world spins together, an awkward ballet,
With confetti confessions, come join in the play.

Through all of our follies, with flair and with jest,
Like clowns at a circus, we give it our best.
In every elastic twist, hugs from afar,
We're joined by our laughter, our own shining star.

So here's to the antics that bind us as one,
In a tapestry bright where humor is spun.
With laughter our anchor, come dance in our band,
In this circus of life, we're hand in hand.

Unraveled Paths

In a world of tangled strings,
Socks lose mates like lost kings.
Cats chase tails, dogs dig holes,
Who knew order's for the trolls?

Spaghetti sprawls upon my plate,
Forks and knives in food debate.
Noodles twist in funny dance,
Oh, the chaos, not a chance!

Paperclips are heroes bold,
Holding dreams that won't grow old.
But in the drawer, they just fight,
They'll unite when it's bedtime light!

Maps with routes that don't align,
GPS says, "You'll be just fine!"
Yet every turn's a brand new quest,
Like finding socks, this is a test!

United Souls

Beans in a pot, oh what a stew,
Each flavor beams, but they argue too!
Chili peppers spice up the chat,
While sour cream just sits and chats.

Tree branches dance, swaying around,
They gossip softly without a sound.
Roots mingle deep in the ground,
Nature's crew all tightly bound.

A cat and dog, the folks they tease,
Swapping tales while sipping breeze.
Together they plot, not-so-sneaky,
A plan to steal food; oh, so cheeky!

In the end, we're all a bunch,
Of funny quirks in a wild crunch.
United souls from coast to coast,
Laughing together, that's the most!

The Interwoven Story

Once upon a tangled yarn,
Knitting tales of joy and charm.
Every stitch, a laugh or tear,
The cat leaps in, now threadbare!

A quilt is made with bits and scraps,
Each patch a tale, oh, how it wraps!
Grandma's stories in every seam,
What's that — a rat? Oh, it's a dream!

Baking cookies, flour flies,
Silly shapes meet giggly pies.
Oh, what fun it is to make,
Just don't forget the sweet mistake!

Each person builds their tale with flair,
Like socks that vanish in the air.
We weave together with a smile,
The interwoven story, all the while!

Bonds Beyond Borders

The panda laughs while munching bamboo,
While kangaroos play leapfrog, it's true!
A penguin waddles, slips with style,
Now that's a moment worth a while!

Across the seas, a cat takes flight,
From Paris to Rome, oh what a sight!
With cheese and wine, they toast so loud,
The world's a stage, and they're so proud.

Worms and birds, oh sweet duet,
In gardens grand, who could forget?
The laughter of bugs fills the air,
Creating bonds beyond compare.

As the sun sets on distant lands,
We join the fun with open hands.
It's a silly dance of hearts that soar,
Making friends forevermore!

The Harmony of Humanity

Balancing acts on a tightrope thin,
Juggling dreams with a silly grin.
Each laugh, a note in the song we sing,
In this harmony, the joy it brings.

Dancing trees with arms so wide,
Invite the world for a joyful ride.
Frogs croak tunes like it's a show,
While fireflies dance in the glow.

Balloons float high without a care,
Chasing clouds that drift and share.
A conga line of hearts in bloom,
In every corner, love finds room!

So let's embrace each quirk and flaw,
Celebrate life with a shiny jaw.
From every land and every face,
We find our rhythm, our happy place!

A Mosaic of Lives

In a park where the squirrels all chat,
A dog winks at a cat in a hat.
They swap tales of food and of snoozing,
While pigeons plot some lively cruising.

The sun spills laughter on the grass,
As kids race by, and the moments pass.
An old man coughs, then starts to dance,
While children giggle at his odd prance.

A couple shares a hotdog delight,
With mustard fights that ignite the night.
All around, differing folks combine,
Creating a chaos that feels divine.

In this lively blend, the world feels bright,
With each quirky soul, there's pure delight.
From balloons to banter, all still alive,
Together they flourish, all thrive and jive.

Threads of Connection

A grandma knits with colors galore,
While ants march by, a tiny encore.
Her cat tries to steal the yarn from her lap,
With every tug, there's a comedic flap.

The mailman's hat flies off in a breeze,
Chased by a dog who's ready to tease.
Neighbors peek out, sharing a grin,
As comedy unfolds, where all can win.

At the café, a cup slides from sight,
Yet lands in a mugger's grasp, what a sight!
Laughter erupts like freshly popped corn,
Welcome to chaos, where bonds are born.

In this tapestry sewn by chance and jest,
Every wild moment feels like a fest.
We dance through life, all quirky and bold,
In a funny world, together we hold.

Unity's Embrace

A snail in a hat, quite the odd sight,
As it races a turtle, side by side in flight.
With cheers from the birds on a low-hanging wire,
This funny parade is surely a quire.

Two goats on a hill, planning a scheme,
To steal all the flowers, it seems like a dream.
With a flick of their tails, they charm us so grand,
Life's absurd antics in this merry land.

A grandpa trips over a cat on the prowl,
And they end up laughing, both sharing a growl.
Their bond only strengthened through silly mishaps,
As animals join in, sharing funny claps.

Together they dance in a whimsical whirl,
Merging each blunder, boy, ain't life a pearl?
In each silly moment, united we prance,
Finding joy in the chaos, a hilarious dance.

The Fabric of Existence

A juggler drops pies, oh what a display!
As the crowd roars and starts to sway.
Balloons get entangled with laughter so bright,
In this tapestry spun from pure delight.

A poet slips, dropping his pen with a clatter,
As everyone giggles, wondering what's the matter.
But poetry lives in the dance of the day,
Each slip and trip just adds to the play.

A kid with a kite that knots in a tree,
He yanks and he pulls, bursting with glee.
All together, they pull, and the kite takes flight,
Creating a spectacle, a joyful sight.

With colors of laughter, we weave and we blend,
In this fabric of life, there's always a bend.
Together we thrive, with quirks we all share,
With joy in our hearts, it's a world full of flair.

A Symphony of Bonds

In a circus of smiles and quirky frowns,
A juggler drops balls and spins round and round.
Laughter erupts like a bursting balloon,
As we all dance to the same silly tune.

A cat snug in a hat plays the flute,
While the frog in a bowtie sings to a brute.
The elephants march with a wobbly gait,
All coming together to celebrate fate.

A squirrel strums strings on a ukulele,
A parody band playing wildly and freely.
The world is a stage, and we all are players,
Filling the scene with our laughter displays.

So let's gather 'round for a goofy parade,
With cheerleaders cheering and clowns in sunshade.
As the circus dissolves into twilight so bright,
We all share a grin in the soft, twinkling light.

The Tapestry of Existence

In a knitting class where the yarn is a mess,
The needles collide, causing more than a stress.
Scarves that once matched now look like confetti,
As grandma grumbles, her patience unsteady.

A cat with a sweater? It's quite a sight!
Though one sleeve is longer, it sparks pure delight.
With laughter, they stitch through the fabric of time,
Creating a quilt that's so silly, it's prime.

Errant threads dance like a wild, crazy breeze,
And socks find their partners with magical ease.
In a world of unravels, we still make it whole,
With every stitched smile, we fulfill our role.

So grab your hooks, yarn, be part of the spree,
Let's craft and create, come and join the family!
In this tapestry, odd ends are the treasure,
For laughter's the bond that we all can measure.

Interlaced Hearts

In a cafe where friends sip their tea with a grin,
A waiter spills coffee and starts up a din.
Spoons start to rattle, and laughter erupts,
As the donuts approve of their sugary fluffs.

Two hearts at a table, both plotting to bake,
One uses salt when the other needs cake.
Mixing mishaps, both sweet and quite savory,
They serve up a dish of pure culinary bravery.

A toast to those blunders, with giggles in tow,
To flavors that clash but still manage to glow.
In a kitchen of chaos, confusion, and cheer,
We find that our hearts beat more closely, my dear.

So come raise your glasses to friendships so true,
With toast and with laughter, we'll find a way through.
For in every recipe, both silly and smart,
Are nuggets of joy that connect every heart.

Bridges of Understanding

Two ants on a crumb make a bridge from a chip,
Their teamwork, a wonder, watch how they grip.
All while a snail makes its slow, steady track,
Claiming it's 'fast' with a wink, looking back.

A penguin with shades waddles across,
While a turtle and rabbit are simply at a loss.
"Let's race!" says the turtle, quite unbothered,
"Your speed means nothing!" the rabbit just hollered.

Belly flops turn into whirlpools of glee,
As fish join the party, so wild and carefree.
With every sweet giggle, our links intertwine,
Creating a bridge where no ends we define.

So gather your pals, be they silly or smart,
We'll build up this laughter and world from the start.
For in every chuckle, we find ways to roam,
These bridges connect us; together, we're home.

Where Paths Converge

Two squirrels race on wires, just for fun,
A dog chases a tail, oh what a run!
Pigeons bask in sunlight, strut their best,
While cats play chess, they never rest.

Bikes and trikes weave through the park,
Laughter echoes as kids embark,
A kite gets tangled in a tree so tall,
Everyone giggles, it's a free-for-all.

Elders share tales, spun with glee,
One says, 'I once climbed a big ol' tree!'
While folks from all walks stroll side by side,
It's hard not to feel that joyful ride.

As night falls gently, stars start to gleam,
People clink their glasses, eyes agleam,
A toast to the mishaps and all the laughs,
To the silly ways life crafts its paths.

The Dance of Togetherness

In the kitchen, spoons fly, pots do sway,
Grandma's cooking tips make a funny display,
Kids dance with pancakes, flipping with flair,
While pets prance around without a care.

Neighbors hop by with quirky treats,
One brings pickles; another, sweets!
They twirl, they twine in this playful mix,
As the clock ticks on, with all its tricks.

In the garden, plants hold hands,
Weeds and flowers join the funky bands,
Bumblebees buzz like they're on a spree,
Creating a buzz, singing out with glee.

The moonlight shines on this crazy dance,
Where everyone wobbles, giving chance,
To laugh, to play, to be in the groove,
In this amusing chaos, we all improve.

Unifying Echoes

A phone's ringtone goes, 'Ding-ding!' so loud,
While a cat meows, feeling so proud,
Kids yelling 'Marco!' from feet to the sky,
Pure joy gathers, like clouds floating by.

Horns honk, as cars form a parade,
Drivers calling out, shaped by the jade,
A skateboarder zooms past with flair,
Creating wild ripples, all find their share.

In cafes, chatter blends like a stew,
'Where's my coffee?' asks one—oh, who knew?
A waitress spins, serves laughter and cheer,
She knows that a smile is worth more than beer.

As the sun dips low, laughter's the sound,
In this big circus, lost and found,
Familiar and new, we dance and we jest,
In echoes of joy, we're truly blessed.

The Connection Quilt

Stitched squares of colors, bright and bold,
Gathering tales that never grow old,
A patch from a picnic, another, a race,
Binding memories, all in one space.

Grandpa brings the laughter, while the kids sow,
Fumbles and giggles make the fabric glow,
A lost pet sock, now part of the mix,
Every stitch helps in knitting our tricks.

From wild adventures to quiet nights,
Every square holds echoes of pure delights,
The fabric whispers stories untold,
Each thread a connection, bright and bold.

With love as the needle, we rise and we play,
Tangles and knots won't lead us astray,
As each patch fits snugly in this grand game,
We're all stitched together, never the same.

In the Weave of Being

In the loom of life, we dance and weave,
Threads of laughter, all hard to believe.
One knot on my shoe, you trip on the cloud,
Together we stumble, oh, isn't it loud?

From noodles to planets, we swing and we sway,
With jokes like spaghetti, we twirl all day.
A tickle from friendship, we giggle and flow,
In the grand tapestry, you're in my show!

A pie chart of chaos, each slice is a grin,
Witty remarks make our heads spin and spin.
A patchwork of antics, we sew with delight,
Watch out, world—here comes our silly flight!

So let's swirl in the mix, merry and bright,
With a wink and a nudge, let's take on the night.
In mischief and giggles, we jump to the beat,
In this quirky ballet, life tastes like a treat!

Bonds of Echoing Souls

In the court of odd ducks, we waddle in cheer,
Each quack is a moment that brings us near.
With spoons made of rubber and forks made of cheese,
We gather our laughter like leaves in the breeze.

Juggling our fumbles, we laugh like the stars,
Playing hopscotch on Jupiter, dodging the cars.
With a slapstick of joy, we trip on our fate,
In the circus of friendship, we're topping the plate!

Bouncing like bunnies on a trampoline high,
Our hearts beat in rhythm, oh me, oh my!
A symphony of giggles, we serenade all,
In our garden of humor, we're having a ball!

So let's crack up the silence, make thunder with glee,
For every small hiccup's a chance to decree:
When life's just a riddle, we'll solve it with grace,
With bonds of echoing giggles, we'll find our place!

The Strength of Interconnection

Like gummy bears tangled in a bright rainbow,
We cling to each other, taking it slow.
A dance on a spoon, a leap over pie,
With syrupy smiles, we reach for the sky!

Through a tumble of giggles and snorts, we attempt,
Finding joy in the chaos, we happily spent.
With quirks that defy all the laws of the wise,
We create our own realms beyond ordinary skies!

In the playground of awkwardness, we swirl like a kite,
Waving our flags as we take flight in delight.
Proclaiming our bond with a bubble-wrap cheer,
We break all the records for loudest of jeers!

So here's to the misfits, the jesters, the fun,
Together we rise, and we shine like the sun.
With each silly moment, we build something grand,
The strength of our glee, the best part of the plan!

Waves of Unity

Surfing on laughter like waves on the shore,
Riding the highs, oh, who could ask for more?
With splashes of whimsy, we paddle in tune,
Kites of our dreams dancing under the moon!

In the ocean of shenanigans, we float side by side,
Crafting our castles with each foolish ride.
The tide brings us close in this nutty parade,
Each wave like a hug is a friendship cascade!

So grab your inflatable, let's race to the sun,
With noodles and dolphins, it's all just for fun.
Together we're silly, like seagulls with flair,
In our whimsical whirlpool, we're free as the air!

With every splash that we make, we invent,
A sea full of giggles, love never is spent.
So ride on the waves, let our laughter unfurl,
In this joyful tsunami, we're all part of the swirl!

www.ingramcontent.com/pod-product-compliance
Lightning Source LLC
Chambersburg PA
CBHW060119230426
43661CB00003B/256